OPTICAL

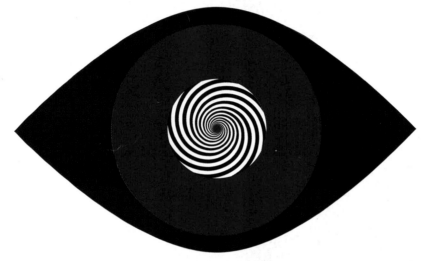

ILLUSIONS

GIANNI A. SARCONE AND MARIE-JO WAEBER

Concepts, text and research: Gianni A. Sarcone

Design and Editorial: Tall Tree Ltd
Project Editor: Harriet Stone

First published in the UK in 2017
by QED Publishing
Part of The Quarto Group
The Old Brewery,
6 Blundell Street,
London, N7 9BH

A catalogue record for this book is available
from the British Library.

ISBN 978 1 78493 847 5

Printed in China

Words in **bold** are explained
in the glossary on page 94.

CONTENTS

Light

Lines and Space

Motion

The Brain

Experiments

IS SEEING BELIEVING?

Can you really believe what you see? This book will show you some amazing illusions that will trick your eyes and brain. The last chapter contains simple experiments to show you how you can make your own incredible illusions.

How You See

At the front of your head are two forward-facing jelly balls, called your eyes. Rays of light are bent as they pass through the cornea and enter your eye through a tiny peephole, called the pupil. The lens bends the light rays a little more to focus them, before they pass through the middle of the eye and hit the **retina**, the lining at the back of each eyeball. As light hits the retina, it stimulates millions of light-sensitive cells, called **photoreceptors**. These send electrical nerve signals along the optic nerve to the back of the brain and a part called the visual cortex. This produces the final images that you see.

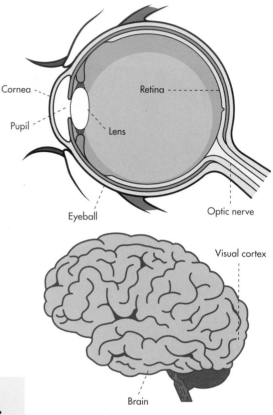

Context

While that all sounds nice and scientific, your seeing equipment can sometimes be fooled into seeing things that aren't there, or incorrectly seeing things that are there. These effects are called optical illusions. Many illusions are created because we don't see objects on their own. Instead, we see them in context and surrounded by other objects which can influence how we see things.

Without any context...

Surrounded by different contexts...

...the two red dots look the same.

...the same two dots look different.

Fooling Your Brain

By playing around with the context of colours, shapes and tones, and by changing the viewpoint of the audience, you can create a wide range of illusions that will have your audience questioning what is real and what is not real!

What colour are this cat's eyes? Turn to page 11 to find out.

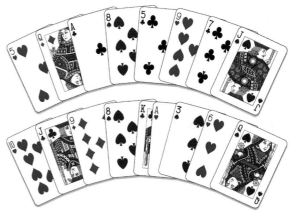

Go to page 26 to see which deck of cards is wider.

Can you see a triangle between the circles? Go to page 52 to find out why.

Page 48 will tell you why this pattern looks like it's moving.

LIGHT

A tiny ant and a giant planet have something in common: they both cast a shadow! Light travels in straight lines, so if its path is blocked by an object, this creates a dark area, or shadow, behind the object.

Your eyes and brain use contrasts between light and shade to define the shape of objects. Your ability to see in three dimensions depends upon how light and shadow are laid out. When you see a surface that has two differently lit areas, your visual system enhances the contrast to see it more clearly. This is called '**lateral inhibition**', and it works so well that it can create a lot of powerful visual illusions!

Scintillating Grids

You will find that the grey blobs are very faint in grid D and almost non-existent in grid A. They appear in grid B, but the effect is strongest in grid C.

what's going on?

These mysterious blobs only appear when the crossing lines are straight, vertical and horizontal. When this happens the contrast between the lines and the black spaces creates a lateral inhibition effect. This occurs when signals from photoreceptors in your eyes conflict with each other, creating the impression of dark blobs where the pale lines cross

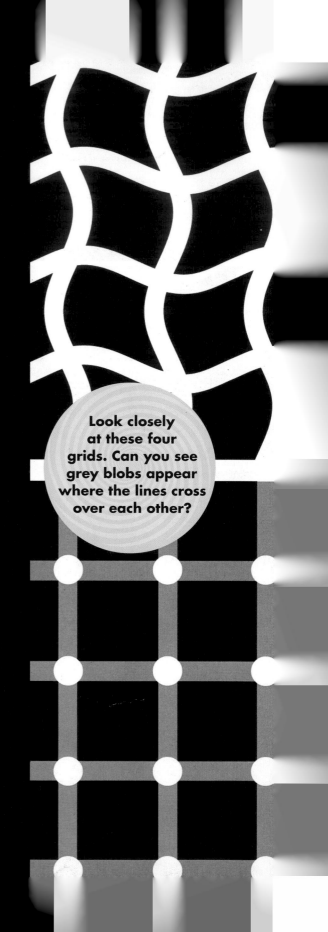

Look closely at these four grids. Can you see grey blobs appear where the lines cross over each other?

Playing With **Contrast**

Look at this cube and its reflection. Which one has darker panels?

In reality, the square panels of both boxes are identical and have exactly the same shade!

what's going on?

This optical effect is called 'simultaneous brightness contrast'. A colour always seems brighter when surrounded by dark colours, or darker when placed on a light background. So the darker background in the reflection makes that cube appear lighter than the cube on the left, which is sitting against a lighter background.

An **Extraordinary Sofa**

Which stripe on the sofa, B or C, has exactly the same grey shade as stripe A?

To check it for yourself, trace the template from page 91, cut out the holes indicated and place it over the sofa so you can see which stripe has the same shade as A.

Stripes A and C are exactly the same shade.

what's going on?

As with the illusion on page 8, this effect is caused by simultaneous brightness contrast, where neighbouring shades affect the apparent brightness of the colours next to them.

Puzzling **Colours**

Colours are not as definite as you might think. The way red looks to you will not be the same as the way it looks to someone else.

Your brain can interpret colours in surprising ways. Because you never see colours on their own, the appearance of any colour is affected by the colours surrounding it. Under certain conditions, colours that are identical may appear different, while colours that are different may look the same.

What colours are the pale bars in between the brightly coloured stripes?

What happens to the pale bars when they are next to two different-coloured lines?

Believe it or not, all the bars on the different striped backgrounds are the same grey colour shown in the top pattern.

what's going on?

This experiment shows the effect of **'colour assimilation'** (see page 18). For example, the grey bars that are next to the blue lines take on a similar tone, and turn bluish. But when the grey bars are next to two different-coloured lines at the same time (as shown by the far column of bars), they look like they have two tones merging into each other.

Colour **Adaptation**

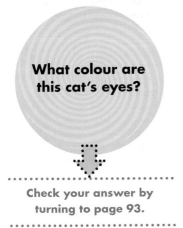

What colour are this cat's eyes?

Check your answer by turning to page 93.

what's going on?

The eye on the right appears coloured because of the purple surrounding it. If you look at the same picture with the purple removed (as on page 93), you can clearly see the grey eye. Thanks to a process called colour adaptation, the purple **desensitizes** the brain to that part of the image. This subtracts a bit of purple from the grey eye, making it appear green.

Restoring **Colour**

Can you make these faded grey parrots look bright and colourful again?

Stare at the bright dot in the striped square below the photo for about 30 seconds. Now look back to the photo and see what happens.

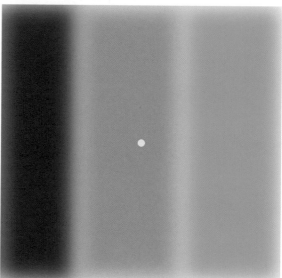

When you look back at the photo, the parrots' colours will have returned.

what's going on?

This effect is caused by colour adaptation (see page 11) and it happens when your eyes take a few seconds to adapt to a light source. As you stare at the striped square, your eyes become desensitized to those colours. So, when you look back at the parrots, they will appear to have **complementary colours** for a few seconds! For example, the blue colour creates a complementary orange **after-image**.

Neon **Colours Effect**

Stare at this electrical circuit for a few seconds and see what happens between the blue lines.

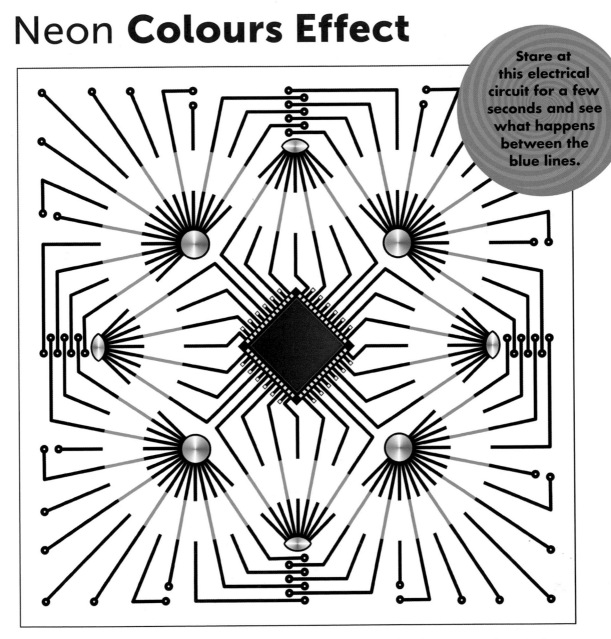

After a while, a bright blue twisting strip appears over the blue lines, even though there is no blue tint on the background (which is actually white!).

what's going on?

This shading effect is called 'subjective transparency', 'spreading neon colour effect' or even 'Tron effect'. It was first observed by Italian researcher Dario Varin in 1971 and it may be left over from when our eyesight first evolved many millions of years ago in the dark depths of the ocean.

Stained Glass Illusion

Take a look at the panes indicated by white arrows. Are they the same colour?

Use the template from page 90 and place it over the stained glass windows to reveal the truth.

When you place your template over the image, you'll see that the two panes are actually the same colour, even though one appears to be green and the other red!

what's going on?

This strange visual effect is known as '**colour contrast**' and shows that the same colour may look very different when it appears against different coloured backgrounds. This happens because our brain increases the contrast of the outline of an object in relation to its background.

Making **Colours**

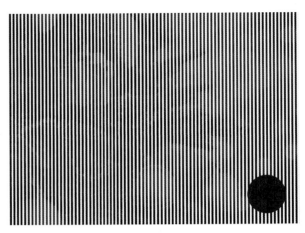

Is it possible to create a full-colour image using just one colour and black?

Image 1 shows a black-and-white image taken using a red filter, and then it has had another red Photoshop layer applied using 'screen' blending mode.
Image 2 shows that same image sliced into narrow stripes.
Image 3 shows a black-and-white image made using a green filter (it will still look grey). Image 4 shows what happens when you merge images 2 and 3.

You might expect to only see shades of pink. Instead, the resulting picture (image 4) appears coloured even though it is only made with red and black lines. Even the Christmas tree looks a little greenish. What is even more surprising is that the decoration balls look gold. Amazing, isn't it?

Rubber **Ducks**

What's happening to the yellow colour inside these ducks?

Stand about two metres away and look at this picture before studying it close-up.

When you stand away from the picture, it looks like the colour fills the duck outlines. But when you examine the ducks closely, you will notice that the yellow is only printed on a small rectangle.

what's going on?

Some colours, like yellow, have a low spatial **resolution**. This means it is difficult to see and define the borders of a yellow shape on a clear background. So, your brain tends to spread any colours out until they fill a dark outline, such as the duck drawings.

Magic **Heart**

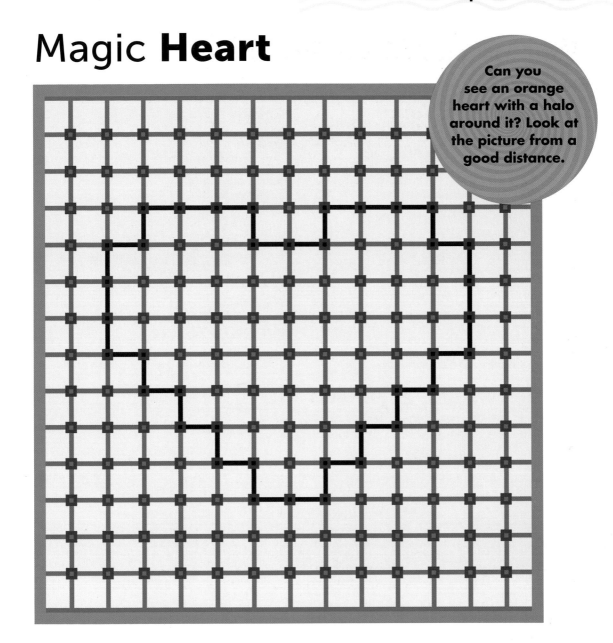

Can you see an orange heart with a halo around it? Look at the picture from a good distance.

what's going on?

The apparent orange heart is created by the interaction of the black lines with the plain yellow background. The halo is formed where blue lines meet the small black squares. Strangely enough, if you really concentrate on the middle of the picture for a while (about 30 seconds) without blinking, you might even see the heart vanish completely!

Playing With **Assimilation**

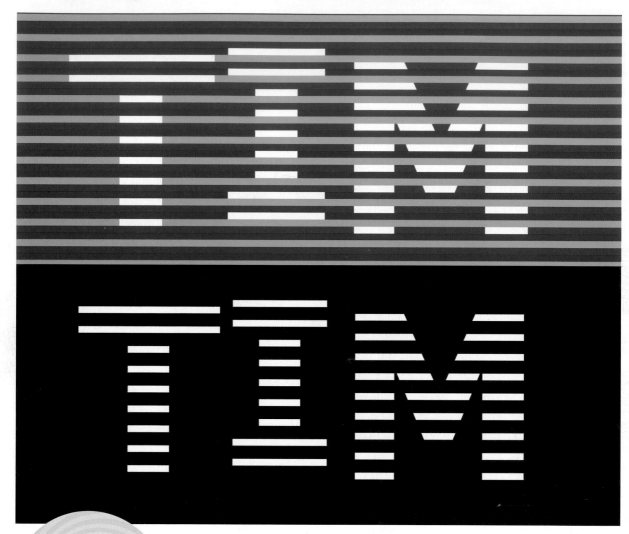

Look at the letters T, I and M in the first image. What colours are they?

The bottom image shows the same letters, with the coloured lines removed.

It looks like each letter is shaded pink, blue or yellow, but they are only made up of horizontal white lines!

what's going on?

This effect is caused by colour assimilation. As with the illusion on page 10, our eyes mix the hues of the two colours around each letter, blending them to form a new shade. For instance, the red and green lines around the white 'M' make it look yellow. Scientists are still unsure why this occurs.

Mapmaker **Illusion**

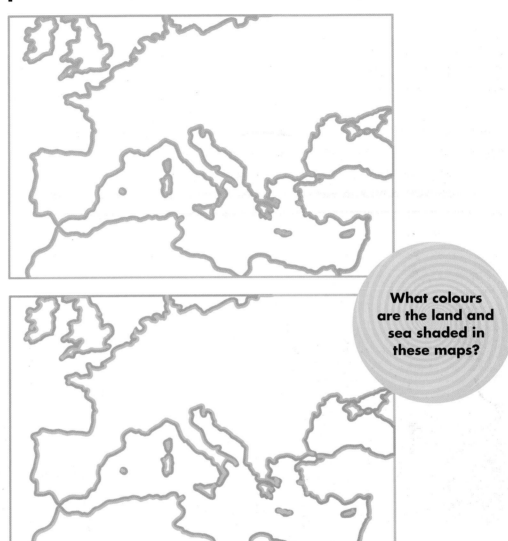

What colours are the land and sea shaded in these maps?

In the top map, the land areas between the orange lines look like they're shaded a pale orange and the sea areas between the blue lines are shaded blue, even though they are both actually white. In the bottom map, the colours and the apparent shaded areas have been reversed.

what's going on?

This illusion, called the 'mapmaker colour illusion', was used by early cartographers to help show one country from another. It is also known as the 'spreading colour' effect. People argue whether this illusion is due to a physical or a mental cause.

LINES AND SPACE

How long? How far away? How much? We measure distances and estimate the dimensions of objects all the time, usually without thinking about it.

We can usually tell the difference between the actual size of an object and its apparent size.

- The actual size of an object cannot be observed (but it can be measured), because it must be viewed from a distance so that your eyes can focus on it.
- The apparent size of an object depends on its size and how far away it is. Objects that are closer will appear larger than if they are farther away.

Perspective and size constancy also play a part in how we see things. They obey these simple rules:

- For two objects with the same ACTUAL size, the one that looks bigger is thought to be closer.
- When we see two objects with the same APPARENT size, the one that appears to be farther away is thought to be larger.

Which line is longer? A or B?

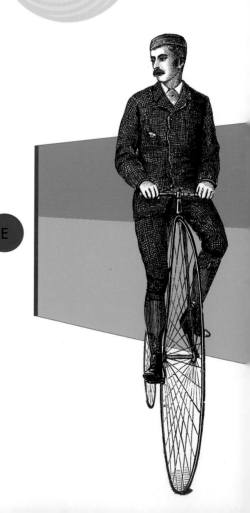

Different Lines

The illusions on these two pages play around with your ideas of perspective and space to fool your brain!

Look at lines C and D. Line C seems to be longer, but are you sure?

Are lines E and F the same length?

In all three illusions, the pairs of lines are the same length as each other.

what's going on?

All the illusions on these pages use your ideas about perspective to play tricks on you. Your mind thinks that the lines that appear to be farther away are bigger when both lines are, in fact, the same size.

Poggendorff's **Illusions**

Which line, blue or green, joins up with the pink line running around the barrel?

Most people (in fact 75 per cent) will say that the blue line joins up with the pink one. However, the correct answer is the green line. Turn to page 93 to see the barrel with the yellow bar removed.

Lining **Up**

Which arrow tail belongs to the arrow head on the other side of the apple?

You may think the pink arrow is the answer, but in fact it is the blue one (check it with a ruler).

Magic **Straws**

Do the red lines on the left-hand straw line up with the green and yellow lines on the other straws?

Only diagonals with the SAME colour are linked by a diagonal line (check it with a ruler).

what's going on?

All three of the illusions on these pages – where a line is broken by the edge, or **contour**, of another object (such as the yellow bar, the apple, or even the space between the straws) – are called Poggendorff's illusions after the German physicist Johann Christian Poggendorff who discovered them. Scientists are still unsure why this type of illusion happens.

Roman **Temple**

MUNDUS VULT DECIPI ERGO DECIPIATUR

Do the columns of this Roman temple converge or diverge from each other?

The Latin words on the temple mean 'the world wants to be deceived, so let it be deceived'.

The columns of the temple are, in fact, perfectly straight and parallel to each other. Check them with a ruler!

what's going on?

This interesting illusion shows how vertical bars which contain patterns that are tilted to one side can look like they are leaning slightly over.

Tilted **Letters**

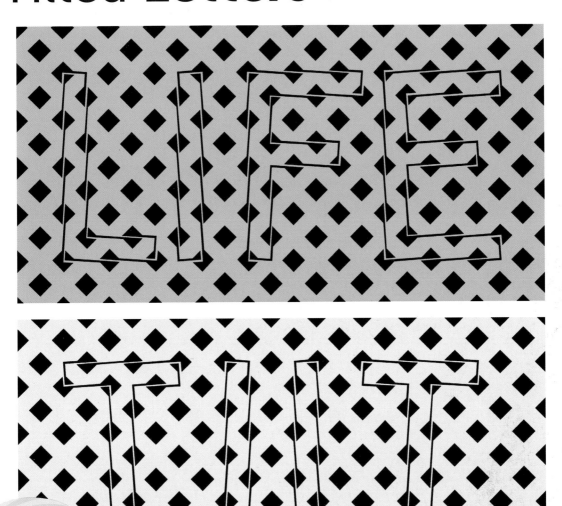

The letters are, in fact, perfectly straight – use a ruler to check.

what's going on?

When a straight line is formed from a number of tilted segments it appears to be tilted itself. This visual effect is called the 'Fraser illusion', after the Scottish psychologist James Fraser, who first described it in 1908.

Amazing **Jastrow**
Playing Cards

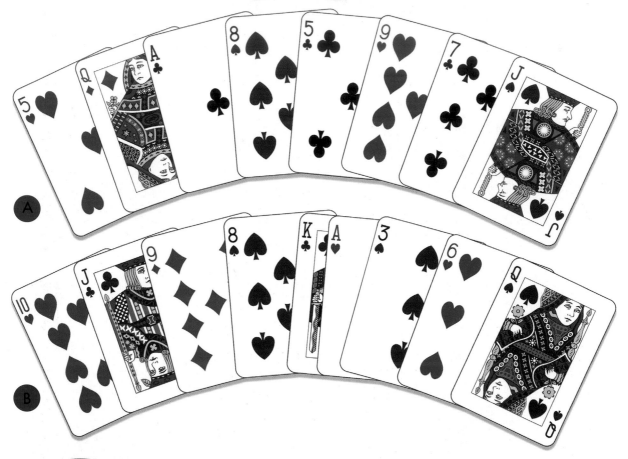

Which of these fanned-out sets of cards is the widest? A or B?

Both sets are, in fact, the same size and width. Turn to page 93 for proof.

what's going on?

When two curved shapes are arranged one above the other as shown here, the lower one always appears wider because your brain believes it is nearer! This illusion is named after the American psychologist Joseph Jastrow. The instructions on page 83 and templates on page 91 will show you how to make your own Jastrow illusion.

Bulging **Shapes**

Do these checked patterns appear to bulge out of the page? And what happens when you add dots?

what's going on?

Because of our assumptions about perspective, our brain assumes that narrow rectangles are farther away than wider rectangles, creating the effect of depth. The small black-and-white dots create the impression of slanting lines which increase the bulging effect.

Wider or Taller?

Is this shirt wider (A to B) than it is tall, or taller (C to D) than it is wide?

Measure both distances with a ruler to check your answer.

The polo shirt may look like it is taller, but actually the width from A to B is greater.

what's going on?

How an object is laid out can affect how you see and interpret it. This visual effect is related to the 'Fick illusion' or 'T-illusion', named after Adolf Eugen Fick, a German physiologist. He described this strange visual effect in which a vertical line appears to be longer than a horizontal one, even though the opposite is true.

Puzzling Hat **Sizes**

Which of these women has the widest forehead?

Use the hat template from page 90 to check your answer.

The woman on the left seems to have a broader forehead than the woman on the right, especially if you look at their faces rather than the tops of their heads. Actually, both women have exactly the same size forehead.

Hidden **Right Angles**

Can you spot any right angles in this puzzling pipework?

There's a right angle in the top right corner of the pipes. It's hard to spot because of the apparent perspective.

Incredible **Circles**

Which of these blue circles is the biggest? A or B?

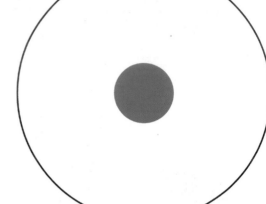

Both circles are actually the same size.

what's going on?

This is known as the 'Delboeuf Illusion'. The bottom blue circle seems larger because it is close to the edge of the outer circle, making it appear 'tighter', and therefore bigger.

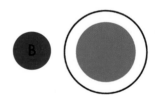

Sarcone's Ellipses

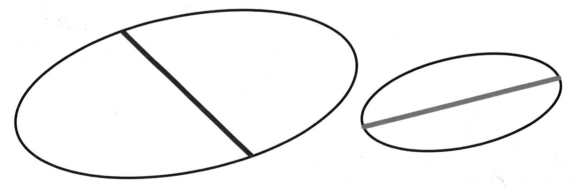

Which line is longer? The red one or the blue one?

what's going on?

Ninety per cent of people will say the red line, but the blue line is actually longer. Your brain gets it wrong because it assumes that the larger ellipse must contain the longer line, so it believes the red line is longer than the blue one, even though the opposite is true.

Bigger or **Smaller?**

Which pink cross is the biggest? A or B? Which pink square is the biggest? C or D?

Most people think that cross A is bigger. However, you may be surprised to learn that crosses A and B are the same size. Similarly, most people believe that square C is bigger than square D, but again, both squares are the same size.

what's going on?

The cross illusion is known as 'Sarcone's Cross Illusion', while the square illusion is called 'Obonai's Square Illusion'. They show that the apparent size of an object can be affected by other objects that are placed close to it, although the effects can vary.

Hybrid **Illusion**

Is this clown sad or is he smiling?

What happens when you step back about two metres and look at him?

When you look at the image close-up, the clown seems sad, but as you step back he will begin to smile.

what's going on?

This type of illusion is known as a cryptic or hybrid optical illusion. It is made by merging two photos with different resolutions. The result is that one of the photos is hidden depending on your distance. When you see the picture close-up, the fine details dominate (the sad clown). When you look at it from a distance, the larger, more blurred tones become visible and the grinning clown appears.

Leaning **Towers**

Were these two photos taken from the same angle?

The towers appear to be leaning more in image A. But the two photos are exactly the same – yet they seem different! You can see proof of this on page 93.

what's going on?

Both photos have the same perspective and the same **vanishing point**. But when they are placed next to each other, your brain interprets them as a single scene with two different vanishing points and it gets confused by the rules of perspective. The leaning effect occurs because the two vanishing points are interpreted as divergent, which is why the tower on the left appears to lean more than the one on the right.

Disrupting Patterns

What's hidden in this black-and-white image?

This black-and-white image contains a black-and-white Dalmatian dog lying on a black-and-white spotted rug (turn to page 93 to see it more clearly).

what's going on?

The dog and the background have been obscured to show how prior knowledge of an object can help you understand an image. For example, you can't see the outline of the dog so you don't recognize it in the image. **Disruptive patterns** like this often occur in nature. The black-and-white stripes of thousands of zebras confuse predators because they cannot focus on an individual animal to catch.

Impossible **Structures**

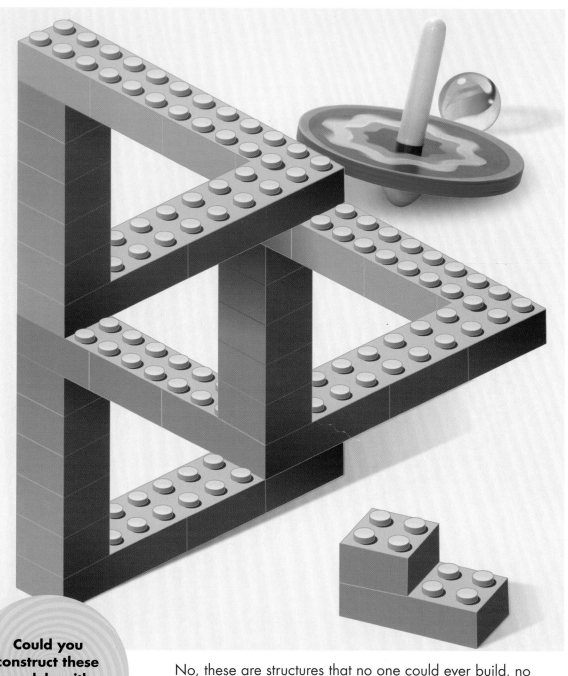

Could you construct these models with building blocks?

No, these are structures that no one could ever build, no matter how many blocks they have. They are known as '**impossible structures**'.

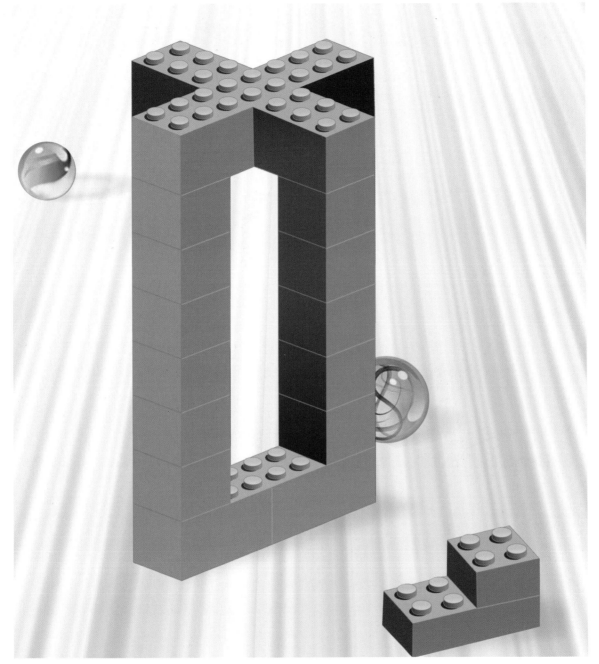

what's going on?

Impossible structures are objects that cannot exist in real life. But that doesn't mean you can't draw them or even create your own illusion of one – the experiment on page 69 shows you how to make your own impossible structure. Generally, when part of an object looks like it's in the wrong place, such as behind, in front, above or below another, then the chances are it is part of an impossible structure.

Impossible **Shapes**

How many prongs does this fork have? Three or four?

It looks like one end of the fork has four prongs, while the other end only has three! Try scanning or copying this picture and then see if you can colour it in. You will soon find that colouring between the lines is a real challenge!

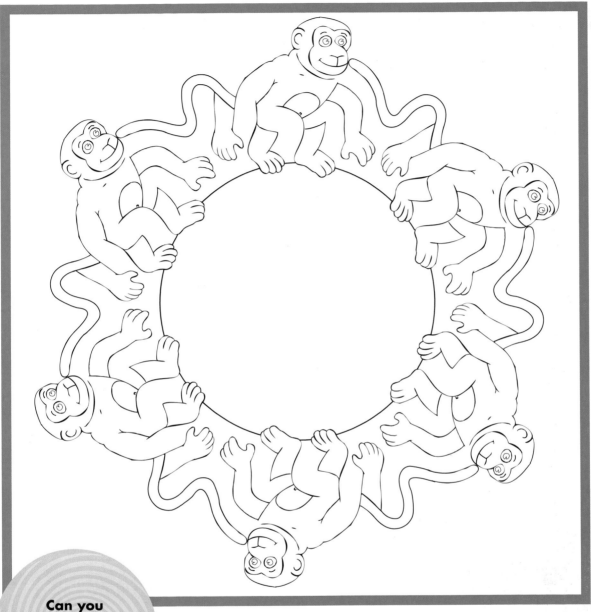

Can you trace and colour in these monkeys?

If you look closely enough at these monkeys you'll see that colouring them in would be impossible as their outlines don't join up! Turn to page 88 to find out how you can create your own impossible animals.

Magic Glass

Can you find a way to magically move the glass off the plate?

Turn the book upside-down and the wine glass will appear to be standing on the table rather than on the dish.

what's going on?

You may also notice that the name on the place card ('Camilla') can be read both ways! Line drawings like this one are known as **ambigrams**, and they can be interpreted differently from various points of view.

Spot the Difference

Can you spot any differences between these women? Turn the book upside-down to check.

When you turn the book around, the woman with the blue glasses looks strange because her mouth and eyes are upside-down!

what's going on?

Your brain is used to seeing faces the right way up, and it is only able to detect small changes in a face in relation to the position of the eyes, the mouth and the nose. When the face is upside-down, your brain cannot process it properly. The interesting part is that the brain thinks it can, so you see everything as correct, until the image is turned around. This illusion is called the 'Thatcher illusion' after former British Prime Minister Margaret Thatcher. Her photo was used to first create this effect by Professor Peter Thompson of the University of York (UK).

Bilateral **Animals**

What can you see here? Ducks, rabbits or dolphins?

The 'Duck or Rabbit' illusion is probably one of the oldest intentionally **ambiguous figures** created for psychological tests. Thousand of variations of the 'Duck or Rabbit' illusion exist. The original illusion (see the image below) is usually credited to the American psychologist Joseph Jastrow who was the first to use it in an article. However, there's every chance it's much older than that!

what's going on?

This illusion is a good example of what scientists call 'rival-schemata ambiguity'. In other words, even though the image is ambiguous, there is no 'dominant' shape, as both images (such as the duck or the rabbit) can be seen at the same time.

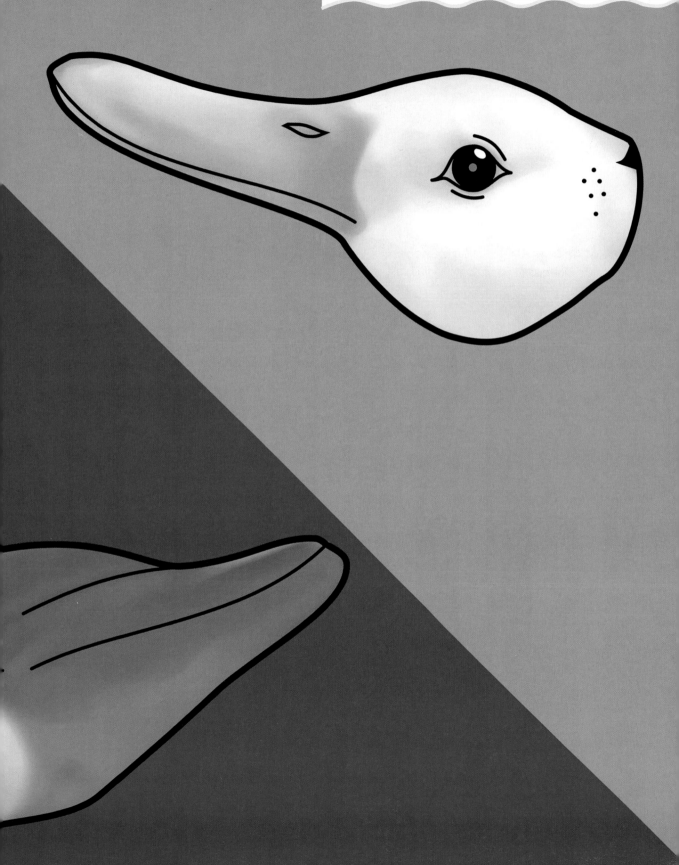

MOTION

Everything moves and everything changes. The Greek philosopher Heraclitus once said: "There is nothing that will always exist, except change." Motion is a part of life. Some objects move very quickly and others so slowly that they seem still – such as a growing tree.

Your eyes are so sensitive to light and motion that, sometimes, you see movement even when there isn't any. This is because your eyes make tiny movements that you are not aware of. When you look at an image you do not actually look at it in a steady way. Instead, your eyes constantly jerk around, locating interesting parts of the scene to build up a mental 'map' of the whole picture. Scientists call these random eye movements '**saccades**'. You can find out how to make your own motion illusion on page 82.

If you concentrate on the circular green rings, you may see a vibrating fluid moving around.

Visual **Flows**
what's going on?

The combination of the black-and-white lines and eye saccades create different after-images. These merge with the green rings, producing a swarm of visual images, which your brain translates into a flowing movement.

Running **Water**

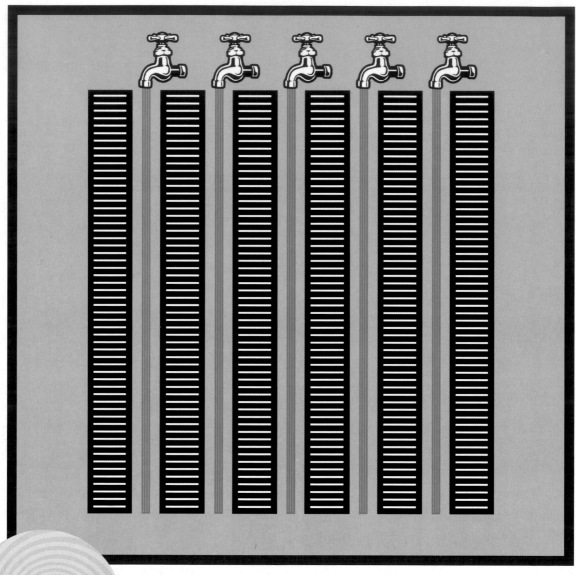

What's happening to the long blue lines?

When you stare at the image, it looks like the lines are twisting up and down, like flowing water.

what's going on?

As you look at this illusion, after-images are produced each time your eye moves. These overlap and compete with the previous after-images, creating an amazing flowing or winking effect. The effect is endless because your eye moves continuously in saccades!

Expanding **Gothic Heart**

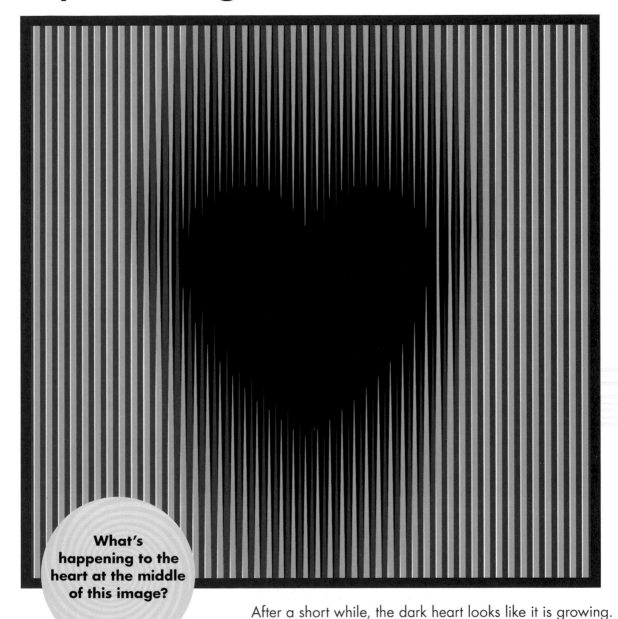

What's happening to the heart at the middle of this image?

Try staring at it then closing your eyes. You will see a white heart appearing.

After a short while, the dark heart looks like it is growing.

what's going on?

The solid central heart is not expanding at all. Instead it is the outer 'blurred' surrounding of thin bright lines that is slowly shrinking because of poor visual stimulus. This gives the impression that the heart is expanding.

Swirling **Whirl**

Does this pattern appear to whirl and shrink?

Try looking at the pattern out of the corner of your eye.

what's going on?

Repeated colour and brightness contrasts can create a feeling of motion. Our visual system, especially our **peripheral vision**, processes bright colours faster than dark colours, and this difference tricks us into thinking that things are moving.

Hovering **Hashtags**

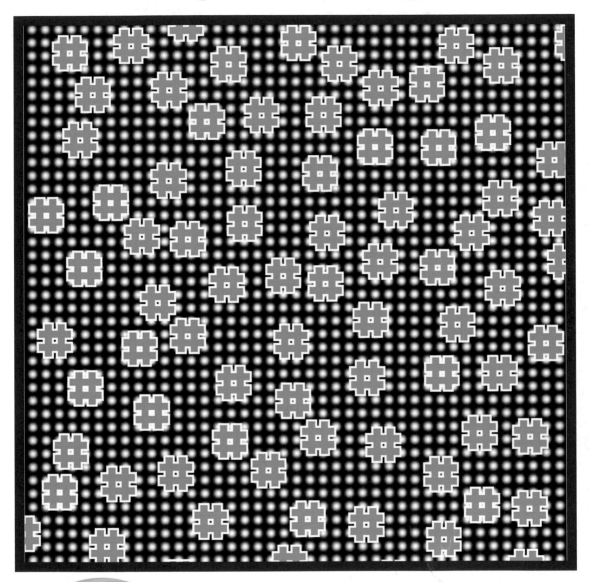

Look at this image for a while. Do the hashtags start to float and swirl above the background?

what's going on?

This happens because our brain interprets the sharp, in-focus images (the hashtags) as being separate from the blurred background. Moreover, most people believe there are two or three different types of hashtag, but there is only one! They look different because the regularity of their shape is disturbed by the background.

Sparkling **Squares**

What happens when you stare at this starry pattern?

As you shift your gaze around this pattern the small dots appear to sparkle.

what's going on?

This sparkling effect is created by the dark beams around the dots and your eye saccades (see page 44).

Pulsing **Star**

Does this blue, red and yellow spiral flash or pulsate as you stare at it?

what's going on?

The pulsating may be caused by differences between your central and peripheral vision. Your **central vision** is sharper and more sensitive to colour, while peripheral vision is sensitive to motion. This difference can create illusions of movement.

THE BRAIN

Without the active involvement of your brain, you would probably see the world as monochromatic (in one colour), upside-down, and with a large hole in the middle.

Your brain is great at filling in gaps in your vision. You may be surprised to learn that there is a hole in the back of each of your eyes. This hole is called the '**blind spot**' and it is where the optic nerve enters the eyeball to connect it to the brain. You don't usually notice this blind spot because your brain is able to reorganize or restore an image to cover up this hole! Your brain applies 'conformation', using incomplete shapes to create lines or contours to fill in the gaps. These are known as **contour illusions**.

Pac-Man Illusion

The Pac-Man shapes in image A give an illusion of a bright white triangle. When the Pac-Man shapes are rotated (image B), the illusion disappears.

what's going on?

In image A, your brain uses the information it is given to form contours that complete the shape: a triangle. This visual effect can be enhanced by adding a grey gradient to the shapes (image C). Now the triangle appears to have a halo around it! In image D, you should be able to see a cat playing with a butterfly, even though the shapes are incomplete. Your brain adds in the missing contours, making the shapes fit with other mental structures that are stored in your mind.

What can you see between these black shapes?

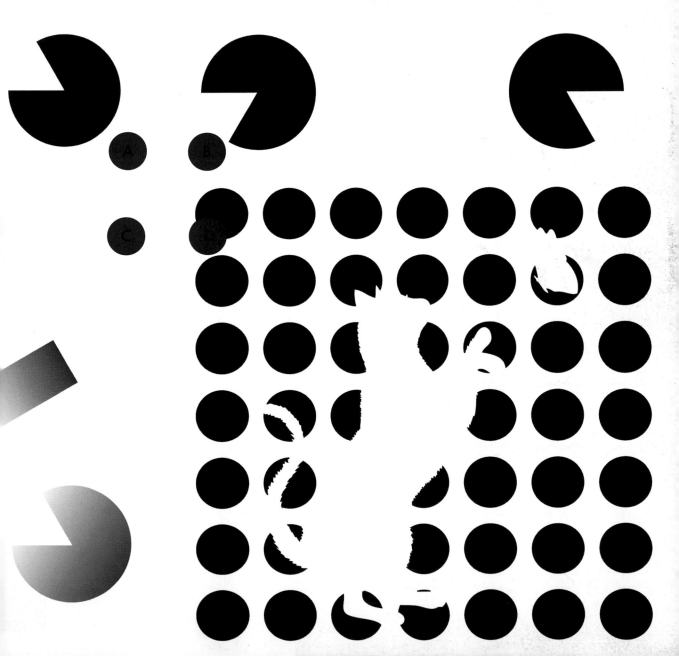

Contours and **3-D Shapes**

See how these 2-D patterns can create the impression of 3-D shapes.

This image looks like a 3-D ball covered with spikes. Even though the overall shape is flat and without contours, your brain interprets the black patterns as spikes sticking out of a sphere!

This looks like a spotted 3-D spring, but where are its contours? In fact, this spring could never exist, because it is only formed from floating coloured discs and semicircles.

Colours Affect **Contours**

The illusions on this page will show you how colours can produce contour effects.

In the pictures above, you may see a pale grey disc in the circle on the left and a bright disc in the circle on the right, even though both backgrounds are white.

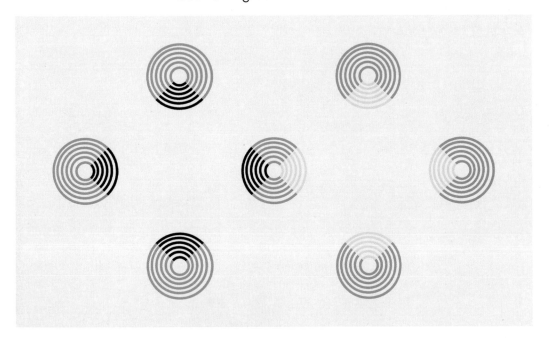

You should be able to see a dark square between the circles on the left and a lighter square between the circles on the right, even though the colour is the same as the background.

what's going on?

In these illusions, the contours are being created by the different colours in the squares and circles. The different colours also affect the tone of the created shapes, with lighter colours producing lighter shapes and darker colours producing darker shapes.

After-effects

'**After-effects**' are visual illusions that appear after your eyes are exposed to a stimulus for a long period of time. There are many types of after-effects. Colour after-effects are usually called after-images.

Can you make the black-and-white image of the cat turn full-colour?

Stare at the small white cross in the coloured image for about 30 seconds. Then quickly shift your gaze to the black-and-white image.

When you now look at the cat on the right, it will appear colourful, but with different colours to the cat on the left.

what's going on?

Staring at a colour for a long period of time will produce an after-image in a complementary colour. Examples of complementary colours are red and green, purple and yellow, and blue and orange. So staring at the blue colour in the image on the left will create an after-effect of orange when you look at the image on the right.

Blurred **Face**

Find out how you can make pin-sharp photos look blurry with this simple illusion.

Stare at the pale star between the upper pair of faces for about 20–30 seconds, then quickly look at the star in the middle of the lower pair of pictures.

You will notice that for just a few seconds the image of the woman on the left will look more blurred than the right one in the bottom pair, even though they are identical.

what's going on?

The illusion comes from a visual after-effect that scientists call 'contrast adaptation' or 'contrast gain control'. It shows that when you look at blurred or unfocused images for a long time, it can affect how you see other objects.

The Mischievous
Leprechaun

1 2 3 4 5 6

Can you make the leprechaun disappear?

Hold the page about 30 centimetres in front of you. Close your left eye and focus with your right eye on each number from six to one, one at a time. Count down as you do this and by the time you get to three, the leprechaun will appear to have wandered off the circle.

what's going on?

The blind spot in each of your eyes has no light-sensitive cells, or photoreceptors. So when the image of the leprechaun enters your blind spot he seems to disappear! French scientist Edme Mariotte was the first person to talk about the blind spot in humans in 1660.

Cheshire **Cat**

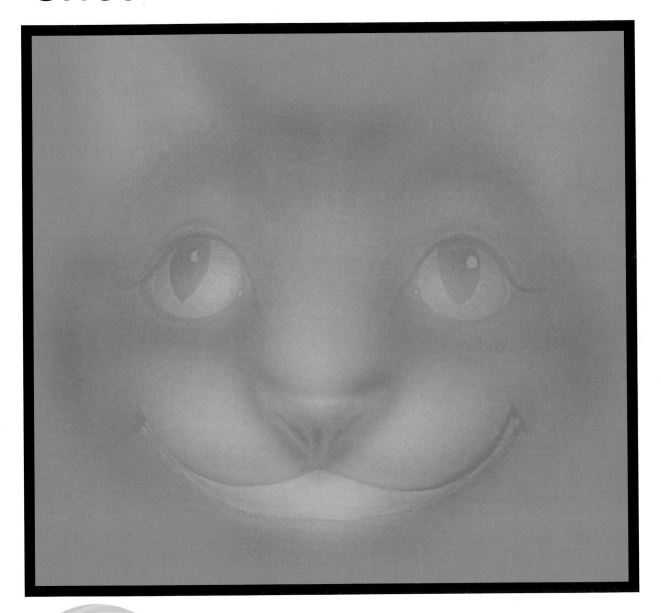

Stare at this cat's nose and count to 20. Watch as the face disappears.

what's going on?

The brown and green colours of the cat are very poor at stimulating your vision, so the image of the cat will appear to fade. Moving your eyes around will restore the image.

Disappearing **Spots**

How many blue and pink spots can you see in this grid of circles?

There are five pink spots and eight blue spots in the picture, but your brain will only let you see a few of them at a time!

what's going on?

When you focus on a single coloured spot, the other ones tend to disappear. This effect occurs because when your eye sees a particularly detailed pattern, your brain may not be able to process all the information it receives accurately.

Broken **Plate?**

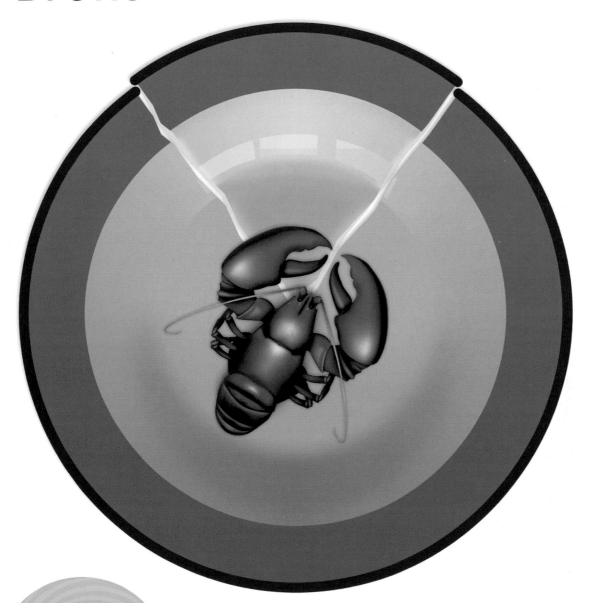

Stare at the lobster's eyes for about 20 seconds and see what happens to the broken plate.

After a while, the rim of the plate will appear to fix itself!

what's going on?

This effect occurs because your brain tends to 'iron out' broken lines in your peripheral vision without you realizing it.

Stereograms;
3-D Wonders

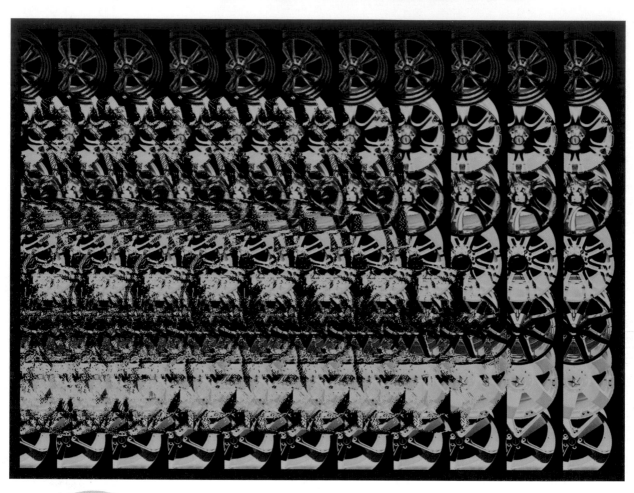

Stare at these coloured patterns. Do 3-D shapes appear out of the page?

Stereograms (also known as 'autostereograms' or 'magic eye') are 3-D images hidden within a 2-D pattern. In order to see the 3-D image, bring the picture close to your eyes, until it touches your nose. At this distance, your eyes cannot focus on the image and they focus somewhere behind the image. Now, slowly move the image away from you, while trying to keep your eyes out-of-focus until you see the hidden image. Seeing a stereogram is tricky and you may have to be patient because it can take a little time.

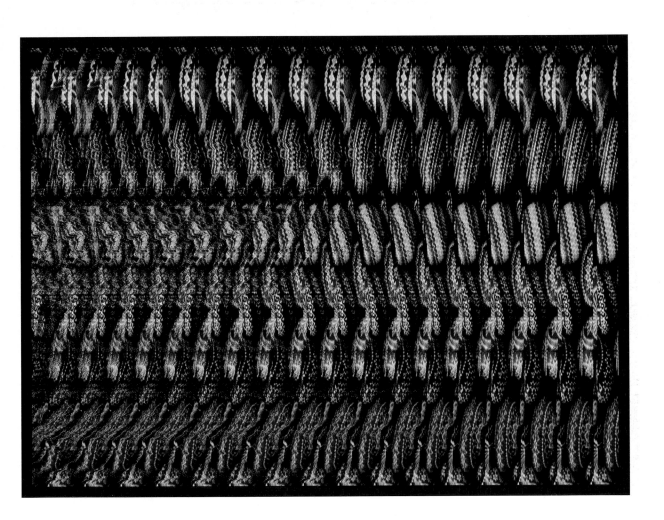

what's going on?

Hopefully you should be able to see a 3-D image of a tricycle in the pattern on the left and a rabbit in the pattern above (you can see them on page 93). When someone looks at a stereogram, the repeating pattern feeds the brain with depth information encoded into it, and the brain perceives the 3-D hidden picture. People with vision problems affecting one or both eyes may not be able to see these 3-D illusions.

EXPERIMENTS

This section contains some simple but effective visual experiments and projects that you can perform at home with your friends and family. You don't need special materials to create illusions that work like magic.

Sarcone's
L-Shaped Puzzle

In the chapter on Lines and Space, you saw how perspective could create illusions. Now use it to fool people with this tricky puzzle.

WHAT YOU NEED

- Sheet of card
- Red, green and blue pencils
- Pair of scissors

1

Trace these L-shapes onto a sheet of card. Colour them in red, green and blue, as shown, and cut out each single piece. You'll notice that the red and green shapes are exactly the same size.

2

Place the puzzle pieces on a table, as shown here, in front of your friends and ask them: which puzzle pieces are exactly the same? Most people will tell you that the red and blue L-shaped pieces are identical.

what's going on?

It is very difficult to estimate the sizes of shapes when they've been skewed like this. The edges, the position and the perspective of the pieces combine to confuse your vision. You can find other illusions that play around with your perspective on pages 20–21.

Remove the Glass from the Tray

Create this magic illusion using what you learned
about the power of line drawings on page 40.

WHAT YOU NEED

- Tracing paper
- Sheet of paper
- Coloured pencils

1 Trace the image showing two glasses on a tray on page 92 onto the paper and colour it in. Then tell your audience that you will move one of the glasses off the tray with a special trick.

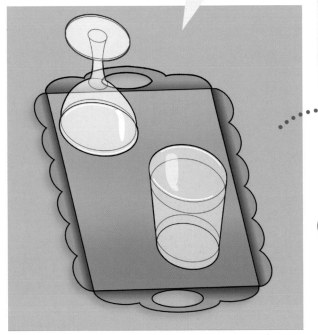

2 Hold the sheet of paper with the picture facing the audience. Fold the picture in half, horizontally.

3 Now, fold it vertically from left to right and towards the audience.

4 Open the rear part of the vertical fold, and then open it horizontally, towards your audience as shown.

5 Listen to the gasps as your audience sees that the wine glass has now moved off the tray – all you've done is turn the image upside-down!

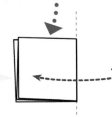

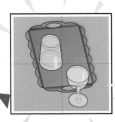

Optics in a **Glass:** Reversing Fish

This illusion uses the power of light to make the impossible possible, or at least to appear that way. But what magical powers lie in a humble glass of water?

WHAT YOU NEED

- Sheet of paper
- Coloured pencils
- Glass
- Water

1 Draw two fish on a sheet of paper and colour in using contrasting colours.

2 Put a clear, empty glass with a round bottom between you and the piece of paper.

3 Partly fill the glass with water. You will see something that you might not expect. The bottom fish is now swimming in the opposite direction! So, how did this magic happen?

what's going on?

This demonstrates a simple physics concept called '**refraction**'. Light bends when it travels through a transparent material. For example, when light rays go through a magnifying glass they bend towards the centre. Where the light rays come together is called the 'focal point', but beyond that focal point the image appears to reverse because the light rays cross over and form a reversed image. This makes the fish appear to swim the other way!

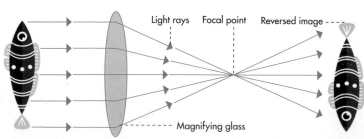

Light rays   Focal point   Reversed image

Magnifying glass

A **Loo Roll** 'Squircle'

In this 3-D illusion you will experiment with an idea based on the 'cylinder illusion' by Japanese engineer Kokichi Sugihara. This particular shape, known as a 'squircle', blends together the shape of a square with the shape of a circle.

WHAT YOU NEED

- Loo roll
- Pencil
- Pair of scissors
- Mirror

1 Squash your loo roll to make it flat. Then open it back out, turn it so that one of the fold lines is running down the centre, and squash it again. Mark three dots about two centimetres from the top, one on the centre fold, and the other two on the outer folds.

2 Using these three points as markers, draw a wavy line. Then, cut the roll along that line.

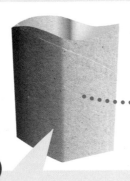

3 Now you have a shape with curved edges, halfway between a rhomboid (square) and a hollow cylinder.

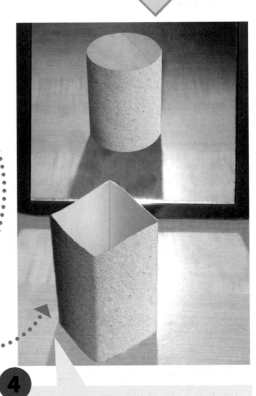

4 Place this shape in front of a mirror and arrange it so that the magic happens! As your brain tends to 'correct' what you see according to your viewpoint, you will see a perfect rhomboid with corners and its reflection as a perfect cylinder.

Playing with **Perspective**

The hybrid illusion on page 32 showed you that things can look very different depending on the location of the viewer. Now try making your own perspective illusion.

1

Photocopy or draw this picture showing a 'broken' pen onto a rectangular piece of paper. Make sure you include the straight shadow as well.

2

Fold the paper in half so that the fold runs through the 'bend' in the pen. Adjust the folded paper so that you get a 3-D impression of a pen standing diagonally between the two sides of the folded paper sheet.

what's going on?

This effect is called '**anamorphosis**'. It uses a distorted image which appears to change shape when seen from a certain angle. Anamorphosis is often used in road markings to make direction arrows and lettering more readable for drivers.

Make an **Impossible** Triangle

On pages 36–37, you saw how playing with perspective produced shapes that couldn't possibly exist. Now find out how to build one!

WHAT YOU NEED

- 14 dice
- Hacksaw
- Glue
- Camera

1

To begin, ask an adult to cut two faces off one of the dice, as shown. They'll need to use a fine hacksaw to create the thin, L-shaped piece.

Ask an adult to help you with this illusion.

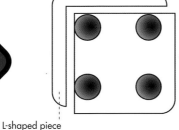

L-shaped piece

2

Glue the rest of the dice together, as shown.

3

Finally, glue the thin, L-shaped piece against the vertical stack of dice.

4

Spin the dice model around and you'll notice that when you reach a certain angle, the three-sided impossible triangle appears. Use your camera to take a photo from this angle (you'll have to get the distance right as well) and amaze your friends with your impossible building skills.

Visual and Mental **Blocks**

Perplex your friends with this 2-D brain puzzle and see how long it takes them to solve it.

WHAT YOU NEED

- Tracing paper
- Sheet of card
- Pencil
- Pair of scissors

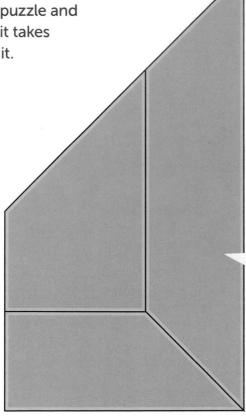

1 Trace these shapes onto a sheet of card. Cut out the three pieces of the puzzle.

2 Ask your friends to make a symmetrical capital letter from these pieces. They are allowed to rotate the pieces as they wish and even to turn them over, but they must not overlap each other. The correct answer is shown to the right.

what's going on?

Your friends will find the puzzle hard to solve because of a mental block. In fact, your brain will tell you to place all the pieces of the puzzle at right angles to each other, making it impossible to solve!

How to **Walk** Through Walls

Find out how a small mirror can give you the power to walk through walls and even fly!

WHAT YOU NEED

• Small rectangular mirror

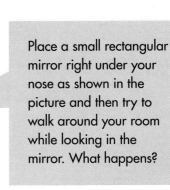

Place a small rectangular mirror right under your nose as shown in the picture and then try to walk around your room while looking in the mirror. What happens?

what's going on?

After a short time, you will feel that what you are walking under is actually right in front of you! You may feel that you are walking through solid objects or even floating in the air. Mirrors can create feelings of disorientation because they don't reverse an image from left to right, as many people think. Instead, they flip an image from front to back (see right).

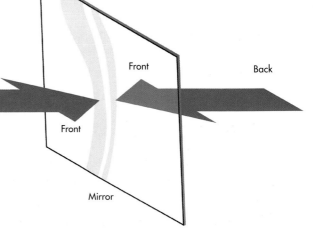

Front   Back

Back   Front

Mirror

Circle to **Square**

Topologists are mathematicians who study strange or even impossible objects, like those on pages 36–39. These 3-D objects include those that appear to only have one side, or even objects that appear linked but actually aren't. This project will show you how a circular shape can hide a square that only you have the power to reveal.

WHAT YOU NEED
- Sheet of paper
- Pair of scissors
- Glue

1
Fold and crease a sheet of paper along its length twice. Unfold the sheet so that you have four creased strips. Cut along the creases to create four thin strips of paper.

2
Glue the strips together in pairs to create two double-length strips.

3
Glue the ends of one double-length strip to create a simple ring. Then glue the other strip to either side of the ring as shown. This creates a one-sided surface – you can draw a continuous line around the loop without leaving the paper surface.

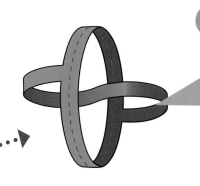

4 Cut along the length of the ring to create two rings of paper. Pass one ring through the other as shown on the right.

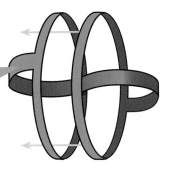

5 Once you have passed one ring through the other, you'll need to turn one of them inside out, so that it has the same orientation as the other ring.

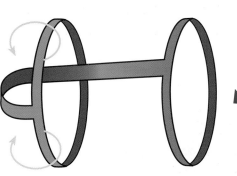

6 You now have what looks like a pair of paper 'handcuffs' (see above). Then, make a cut along the straight strip of paper between the two loops.

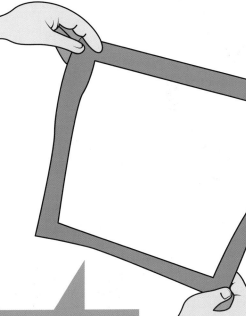

7 Unfold the loops and you'll find that you have turned your loop shape into a square.

Make Your **Own** Hologram Projector

On page 27, you saw how 2-D images could create the illusion of 3-D objects. Now go one step further and make your own 3-D hologram projector.

On page 27, you saw how 2-D images could create the

WHAT YOU NEED

- Graph paper
- Pencil
- Pair of scissors
- Transparent CD case
- Craft knife
- Tape or superglue
- Smartphone

1 Sketch out a trapezoid shape on the graph paper, measuring 1¼ x 4 x 6½ centimetres, as shown below. Then, cut it out to use as a template.

2 Ask an adult to use this template to cut four trapezoid shapes from a CD case with a craft knife. Tape or glue them together to create a flat-topped pyramid.

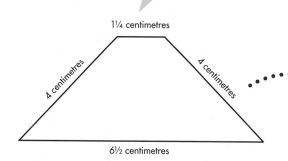

1¼ centimetres

4 centimetres   4 centimetres

6½ centimetres

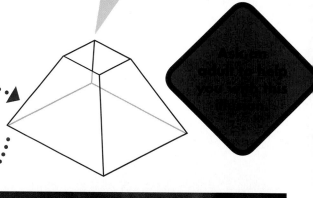

3 Using the web browser on your smartphone, search for 'four-way holographic video' or 'hologram video for pyramid' and choose the hologram you want to show.

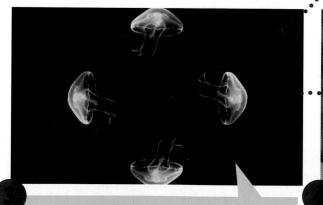

4 With the video playing, place the plastic structure with the smaller base downward onto your phone screen to create a magic, mirrored, 3-D hologram that will amaze your friends!

Hypnotic Disc

Change how your friends view the world by creating your very own hypno-disc.

WHAT YOU NEED

- Paper
- CD
- Glue
- Marble

1 Photocopy and cut out the spiral-shaped template from page 90 and cut out the centre circle.

2 Glue the spiral onto a CD as shown.

3 Glue the marble into the CD's hole and your hypno-disc is ready. Grip the central marble, spin the disc and ask a friend to focus on the spiral for as long as it spins and then look at their hand as soon as it stops. Your friend will be surprised to see their hand bulging!

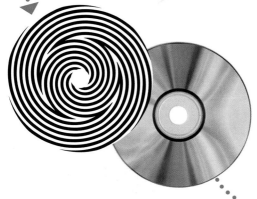

what's going on?

This effect is caused by visual adaptation. Staring at the strong spiral pattern produces an after-effect that alters how you see other objects for a short while. You can find other examples of this effect on pages 44–45 and 56–57.

A **Confusing** Sign

Which way do the fingers point? Confuse your friends with this topological puzzle.

WHAT YOU NEED
- Sheet of paper
- Coloured pencils
- Pair of scissors
- Lollypop stick
- Glue

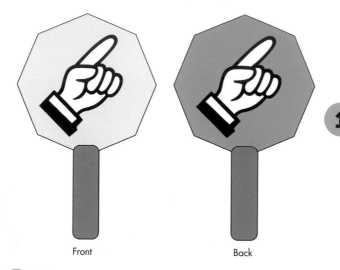

Front   Back

1

Copy the pointing fingers and coloured backgrounds shown here onto paper and cut out the octagons. Glue them back-to-back to the end of a wooden lollypop stick to create your pointing sign.

2

Then ask someone to guess which direction the finger at the back of the sign points when the sign is upright and tilted at 45 or 90 degrees. This is not so obvious and your audience may be surprised at the results.

3

When the sign is tilted at 45 degrees, the finger at the back of the sign points at a right-angle to the finger on the front! And when the sign is tilted at 90 degrees, the finger is pointing in the opposite direction.

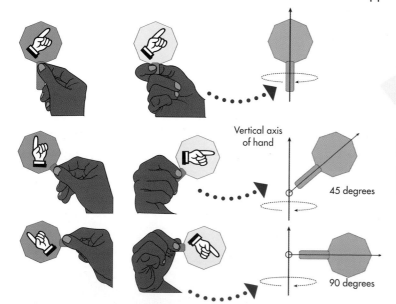

Vertical axis of hand

45 degrees

90 degrees

what's going on?

To understand why this happens, you have to think about the vertical axis of your hand holding the sign, and the axis of the sign's handle. Rotating your hand moves the axis of the sign, making the fingers appear to point in different directions.

Dark Spot, Bright Spot

When you move a grey disc over a background with a changing shade, it will look darker or brighter, depending on its position!

WHAT YOU NEED

- Computer
- Free vector drawing software, such as Inkscape or Vectr
- Printer and paper
- Pair of scissors

1

Using your vector drawing software, draw a large rectangle with a linear grey gradient, which runs from solid black to white. Also draw a light grey disc. Print and cut these out.

Ask an adult before you download software from the internet.

2

Now, place the grey disc onto the linear gradient, and move it slowly from the black end to the white, as shown above. You'll see that the disc appears to get darker as it moves towards the paler background.

what's going on?

This phenomenon is described as 'simultaneous brightness contrast'. This is related to 'lateral inhibition', an effect that enhances the contrast of the outline of an object compared to its background. You can see examples of this on pages 8–9. It is called 'lateral inhibition' because each photoreceptor in our eyes tends to inhibit the response of the ones next to it.

Footstep Illusion

See how changes in contrast can create an impression that objects are walking across the page.

WHAT YOU NEED

- Black pen
- Sheet of paper
- Pair of scissors
- Sheet of transparent plastic
- Blue and yellow coloured paper
- Glue

1

Draw a regular pattern of black stripes with even spaces between them onto the paper as shown here.

2

Cut out a rectangular shape from the transparent sheet and glue on two square pieces of coloured paper, a dark blue one and a yellow one. The squares should be bigger than the thickness of a black stripe.

3

Take the transparent plastic with the coloured squares on it and slide it slowly over the stripes. As you stare at the squares, you'll notice that they appear to take steps, appearing and disappearing as they move over the stripes.

what's going on?

When the dark blue square slides over a black stripe it seems to merge with the stripe and there is no more motion cue that your eyes can see, so your brain interprets it as standing still. The same occurs when the yellow square passes over the white spaces. That's why they seem to stop and move alternately.

How to 'Levitate'

'Levitation' is the miraculous ability to float in the air without any assistance. People from all over the world have claimed to possess this power. Now you can learn how to trick your friends into believing you can levitate too.

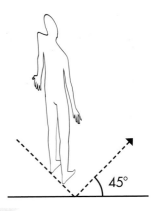

The trick is to position yourself at an angle to your audience – generally 45 degrees. They should also be standing a little distance away, so that they can only see the back part of your far foot and most of your near foot. Try to keep your audience numbers quite small, and make sure that they are standing close together.

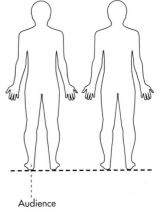

Audience

Then, with your heels held together, lift the whole of the near foot and the back of the far foot off the ground, while standing on just the toes of your far foot. Make sure you also keep your ankles together.

When 'landing', try to make a point of hitting the ground hard with your feet and bending your knees to convince the spectators that your feet really were off the ground.

what's going on?

The audience will only see the heel of your far foot and the whole of your near foot off the ground. This is enough to create an illusion inside their brains that you are levitating.

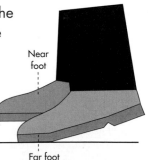

Near foot

Far foot

Photographing **Levitation**

This trick will make your friends believe that you can float in mid-air, using a sponge, some water, and a well-positioned camera.

WHAT YOU NEED
- Water
- Sponge
- Camera

1

To capture the feat of levitation with a camera, first you need to make a dark patch on the ground. Take a wet sponge and dab it gently on the ground. Try to make a damp patch that matches the shadow of you standing. If the patch is too wet, it will look too dark and the illusion won't work, so let it dry a little.

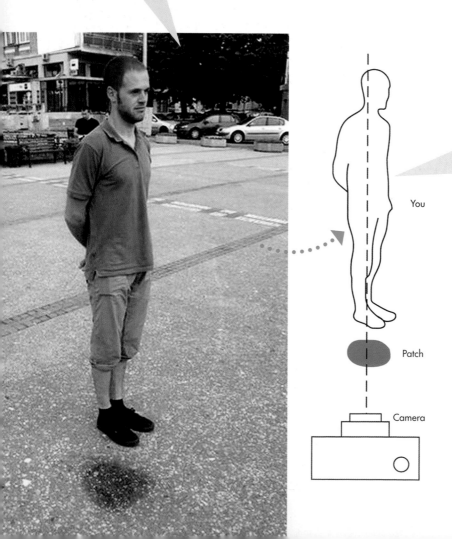

You

Patch

Camera

2

Now stand a short distance away (about 30–40 centimetres) from this damp patch and ask a friend to take a picture from the other side of the damp patch. To get the best effect, you must choose a location and weather conditions where your body doesn't cast a REAL shadow! You may need to move around the patch a little to get the best photo. Once your friend is happy with the effect, he or she can snap away while you are 'levitating'.

Making **Magic** Dice

As with the hybrid illusion on page 32, this visual trick depends on the point of view of the spectators. Just make sure they are standing close to you for this illusion to work.

WHAT YOU NEED
- Two dice
- Small mirror
- White correction fluid

1

Before you start your performance, you will need to 'prepare' a die by painting correction fluid on some of the pips.

Top view

Side view

Bottom view

2

Only paint the pips on four faces of the die, as shown, and make sure you only paint the bottom half of each pip.

Normal die

Prepared die

3

Ask a spectator to examine the normal die, and place it on the mirror – everyone can see the black pips reflected in the mirror. At this point, ask another spectator to take a closer look at the mirror and while he is doing this, secretly swap the normal die with the prepared one. Now, when you lay the prepared die on the mirror, make sure that the number two is facing up. The die will seem normal viewed from above, but its pips have turned WHITE in the mirror!

Moving **Pictures**

To draw a self-moving illusion, like the one on page 48, you may need to use vector drawing software. This will help you to create and position a repeating pattern quickly and easily.

WHAT YOU NEED

- Computer
- Free vector drawing software, such as Inkscape or Vectr
- Printer and paper

1

In a rectangle – the 'cell' – arrange a series of contrasting colours including black and white, in stripes, as seen above. For the background, select a neutral colour, such as light grey.

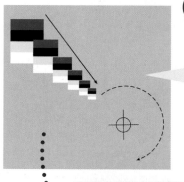

2

Reproduce the cell so that there are six of them, reducing the size by about 20 per cent at each step. Arrange these cells in a diagonal line as if they were radiating out from the centre of a circle, as shown.

3

Copy the line of cells and repeat them to create a complete circle. Now the radiating colour pattern seems to rotate and expand when you look at it. This type of illusion is called 'Peripheral Drift Illusion' because it works best when you use your peripheral vision and don't look at it directly.

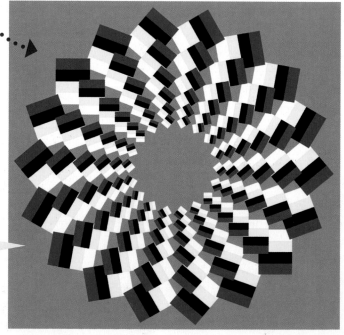

Jastrow **Magic** Experiment

This optical illusion is named after the American psychologist Joseph Jastrow who first discovered it.

A

B

WHAT YOU NEED

- Sheet of card
- Pair of scissors
- Coloured pencils

1

Onto a sheet of card, trace or photocopy the templates on page 91 of the curved shapes showing dolphins, and cut them out. Colour them in contrasting colours using the pencils.

2

Place the two dolphins on a table, with dolphin A on top as shown, and ask a friend to pick which one of them is longer. Most people will say that they look the same size. However, the dolphin in shape A is actually bigger!

3

To prove it, take dolphin B and move it above dolphin A. It's now obvious that one of the shapes is indeed longer than the other.

what's going on?

This illusion is created by your prior assumptions about perspective as described on page 20. You can find a similar Jastrow illusion on page 26.

The Unpredictable **Structure**

Follow these instructions to turn an impossible shape into an unpredictable structure, similar to the one you made on pages 72–73.

WHAT YOU NEED
- Sheet of paper
- A pair of scissors
- Glue

A

B

B
Glue

A
Glue

1

On the sheet of paper, draw the cross-shape shown on the left and cut it out. Join the ends labelled A to make a loop and glue them together. Next, bend the two ends labelled B giving one end a half-twist, and glue them together.

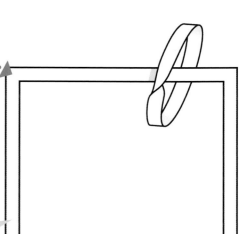

2

Cut all along the blue dashed lines first, to cut the twisted loop into three strips. Then, cut the other loop along the grey dotted line.

3

Open up the paper shape to reveal a small ring locked into a square frame! If you cut the small ring along its length, you would create a twisted figure-of-eight-shaped paper ring!

Hole in the **Hand** Illusion

This simple illusion will give you the impression that you can see right through parts of your body!

Hold the tube in your right hand up to your right eye like a telescope. Now hold your open left hand, with its palm toward you and its edge against the tube, in front of your open left eye. Focus both your eyes ahead and both images will merge into one. Slide your left hand along the tube until you see a hole in the centre of your palm.

WHAT YOU NEED

- A magazine or sheet of card rolled into a tube and held in place with a rubber band

what's going on?

This effect is caused by binocular vision. Each of your eyes receives a different picture and your brain merges these together to create the hole in your hand.

Geometric Illusion

See how arranging these simple geometric
shapes can make part of an object 'disappear'.

WHAT YOU NEED
- Card
- Coloured pencils
- Scissors

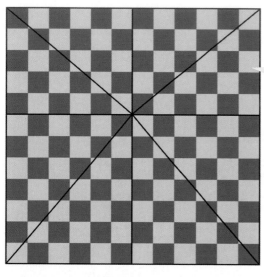

1

Trace the two large squares
shown here and cut them
along the black lines to make
12 triangle and square pieces.

2

Arrange these pieces to form square A shown
below. Then rearrange the shapes to show
square B. Part of the square appears to have
disappeared, even though you're using the
same shapes and the squares are the same size!

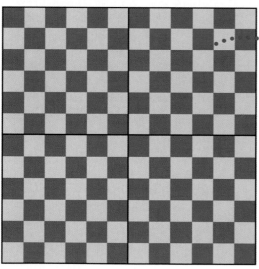

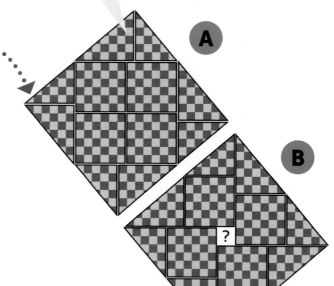

A

B

what's going on?

Actually, square A is not really a square but a slightly concave
shape, whose edges curve inward. Square B with a square hole
in its centre is slightly convex and its edges curve outward. So the
missing section is simply spread along the edges of the square.

Impossible **Triangle**

Pages 36–37 showed you shapes that are impossible to make. Now challenge your friends to create this seemingly impossible triangle from a sheet of paper. Then follow these steps to show them how it's done!

WHAT YOU NEED
- Sheet of paper
- Pair of scissors

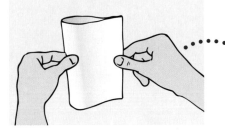

1

Make a short crease across the middle of the paper by pinching the central part only.

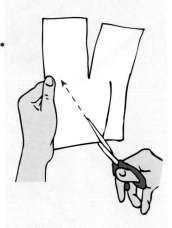

2

Reopen the sheet and make a right-angled cut from the middle of one edge to the centre crease. Then make two cuts to form a V-shape from the opposite edge as shown.

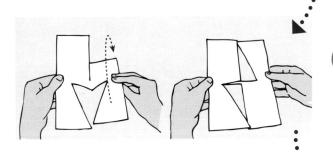

3

Finally, turn the right flap of the sheet forward 180 degrees and the triangle piece should stand upright.

what's going on?

It is amazing how many people aren't able to make this 3-D triangle! The mental block is caused by the fact that we perceive the paper as just a 2-D shape rather than a 3-D object that can be moved and altered.

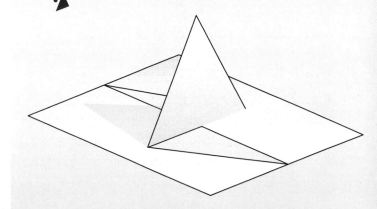

Polypodous Elephants

You saw impossible monkeys on page 39. Now find out how you can create your own impossible elephants.

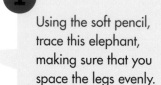

1 Using the soft pencil, trace this elephant, making sure that you space the legs evenly.

2 Erase the elephant's feet and draw them again, but this time add them to the space between each leg, as shown.

3 Trace this new elephant and reproduce it to form a circle, with the tail of one elephant in the trunk of another. Use the pen to define the outlines and then colour the elephants as best you can.

Drawing **Impossible** Stairs

Follow these instructions to draw some stairs you could never climb.

1

Using the soft pencil, draw a stair with three steps as shown.

WHAT YOU NEED

- Soft pencil
- Sheet of paper
- Eraser
- Coloured pencils

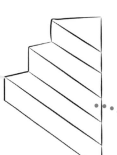

2

Extend the treads and the risers to produce a spiral staircase to one side.

3

Erase the vertical line that divides the two halves of the staircase. Now it looks as if the treads of the stairs on the left are blended with the risers of the spiral stairs.

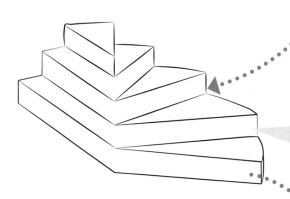

4

Add solid colour to the treads of the spiral stair. You'll produce the best visual effect if you shade the treads of the left stairs with the risers of the spiral stairs so that they blend into each other. You can even add some objects, people, or animals to enhance the illusion.

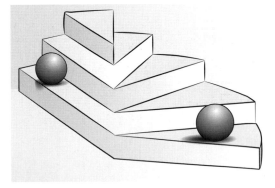

TEMPLATES

Use these templates to check how some of the illusions work and to help you create your own.

PAGE 75

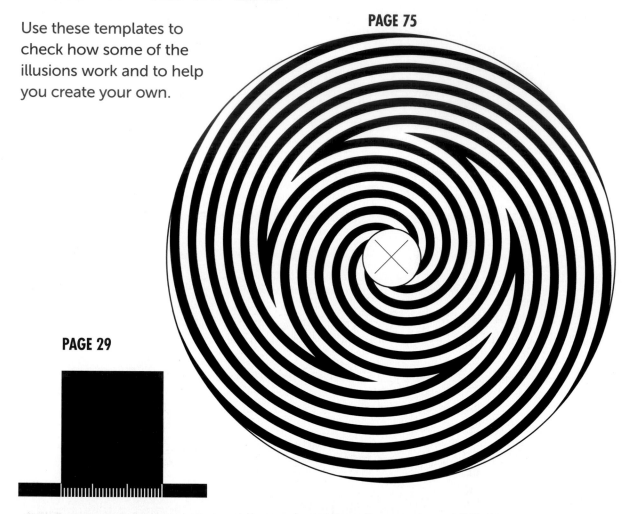

PAGE 29

PAGE 14

PAGE 83

PAGE 9

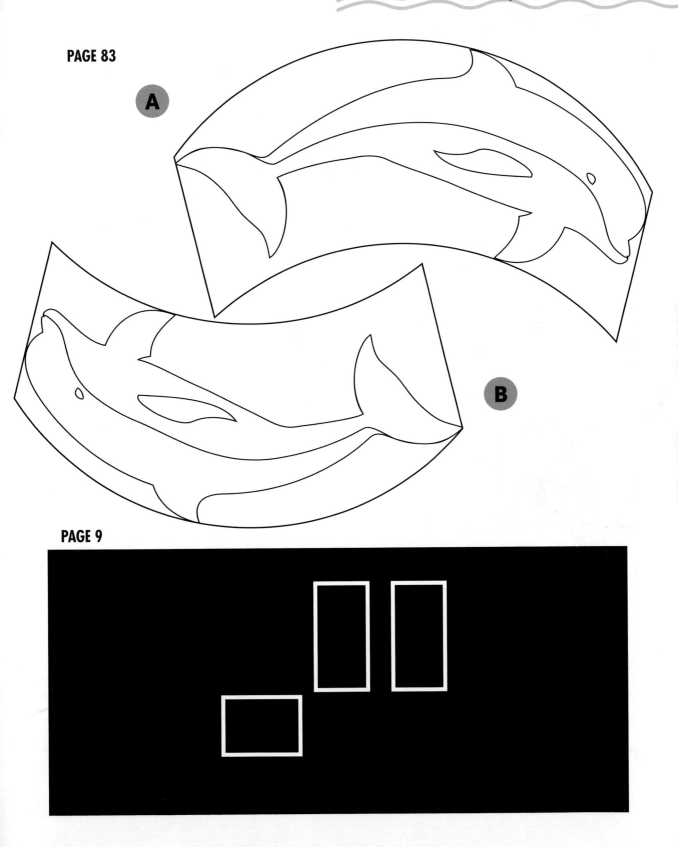

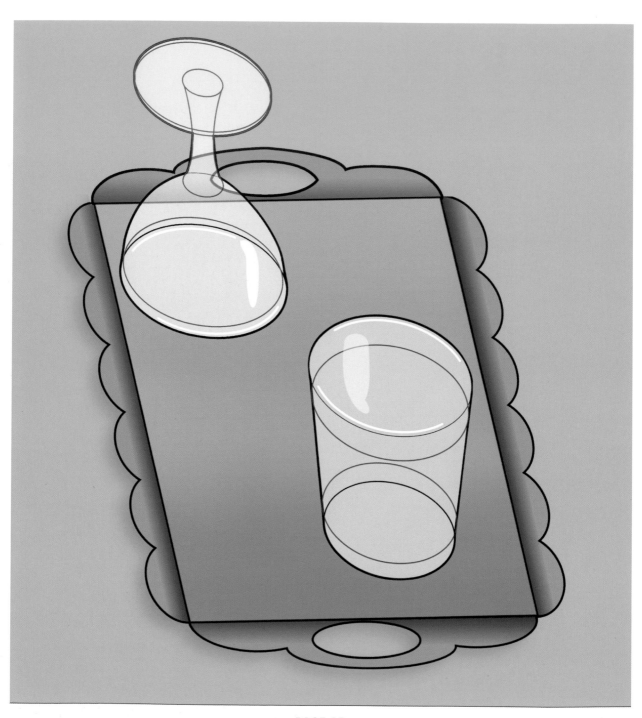

PAGE 65

ANSWERS

These pictures reveal the mysteries of the illusions from earlier in this book.

PAGE 11

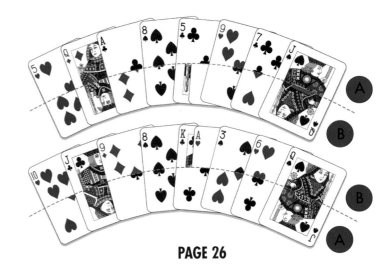

PAGE 26

PAGE 22

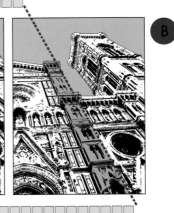

PAGE 33

PAGE 34

PAGE 62

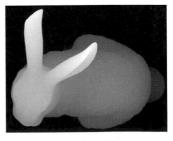

PAGE 63

GLOSSARY

after-effect
An illusion created by your senses being exposed to a stimulus for a long period of time. Colour after-effects are usually called after-images (see below). Other after-effects include a feeling of movement caused by staring at a moving object for a while and then looking at a still one.

after-image
This occurs when you look at brightly coloured images for a long time. The bright colours desensitize part of your retina at the back of the eye. When you look away or at a neutral surface, such as a white page, a ghostly version of the same image appears, but with different colours.

ambigrams
Graphics or words that can be read in more than one way. For example, a word written in such a way that it can be read the right way up and upside-down.

ambiguous figures
These are images that can be interpreted in more than one way.

anamorphosis
A distorted image that has to be looked at from a certain position or angle to view it properly.

blind spot
The part of the retina where the optic nerve leaves the eyeball and where there are no photoreceptors. This creates a small area where you cannot see anything. Usually, your brain fills in this blind spot so that you do not notice it.

central vision
The part of your vision that relates to the photoreceptors at the middle of your retina. These are stimulated when you look directly at something.

colour assimilation
When the areas of colour in a pattern are very small, the opposite effect to colour contrast can occur and colours can appear to be more like a neighbouring colour. So a small or thin grey pattern may appear bluish when placed next to a blue background or yellowish against a yellow background.

colour contrast
This is the apparent change in a colour when it is seen against different colours. For example, colours may look more vibrant against a background that is a complementary colour, or even paler against a dark background and darker against a light background.

complementary colours
These are colours that are directly opposite each other on a colour wheel, such as red and green or blue and orange. When placed next to each other, these colours can create a vibrant optical effect.

contour
The apparent edge of an object.

contour illusions
The impression of the edge, or contour, of an object that is created by other, incomplete shapes.

converge
When two or more objects move or lean toward each other.

desensitizes
Reduces the effect of something, such as a bright light or a particular color.

disruptive patterns
Complicated patterns that are designed to break up the shape of an object. These patterns can hide an object against its background, such as a soldier's camouflaged uniform, or they can be dazzling to confuse somebody watching, such as the bright stripes on a zebra.

diverge
When two or more objects move or lean away from each other.

impossible shapes and structures
These are objects that can be drawn on paper, but are impossible to create in real life.

lateral inhibition
This occurs when a photoreceptor that has been stimulated by light stops or reduces the activity of photoreceptors surrounding it. Lateral inhibition enhances how well you see areas of contrast and, as a result, the edges of objects.

peripheral vision
The edges of your vision and the areas you can see out of the corners of your eyes.

perspective
The principle that objects will appear to get smaller the farther away they are. Perspective is defined by the horizon or by eye level and by vanishing points.

photoreceptors
Light-sensitive cells in the retinas at the backs of your eyes. They are triggered when rays of light fall on them and send signals to the brain, which turns these signals into the pictures you see.

refraction
When the path of a ray of light changes direction as it passes from one transparent material to another, such as moving from air to water.

resolution
How clearly an image can be seen. Printed images or pictures on a television or computer screen are made up of tiny dots, or pixels. The more dots, the greater the resolution, and the sharper the image appears.

retina
The thin layer at the back of the eye that covers nearly three-quarters of the inside of the eyeball. It contains millions of light-sensitive photoreceptors.

saccades
Sudden movements made by your eyes when you look at something. These movements are fast and random and you have no control over them.

topologists
People who study how objects behave when they are deformed, such as by twisting or bending.

vanishing point
An imaginary point on the horizon where the perspective lines of buildings and other objects come together, or converge. As they get closer to a vanishing point, objects appear to get smaller and smaller, until they completely disappear.

INDEX